THE

DANIEL

A BIBLE STUDY GUIDE FOR MEN

THE BOOK OF
DANIEL
A BIBLE STUDY GUIDE FOR MEN

VINCE MILLER

EQUIP
PRESS

THE BOOK OF
DANIEL

Published by Equip Press, Colorado Springs, CO

First Edition: 2023
The Book of Daniel / Vince Miller
Paperback ISBN: 978-1-958585-23-8
eBook ISBN:978-1-958585-24-5

EQUIP
PRESS

DEDICATION

To men who desire to be faithful from beginning to end (and a warning to those who are not).

CONTENTS

CONTENTS

HOW TO USE THIS HANDBOOK

VIDEOS FOR THIS HANDBOOK

As you navigate this handbook, you will discover that the lessons are designed for use with online videos. These videos are viewable with a membership at our website: **www.beresolute. org**. You can use the videos for individual growth or with a group. Each lesson corresponds with the video of the same title. The best part is Vince Miller has structured the videos to provide relevant content for reflection and discussion so that you don't need hours to prepare. He does the work for you. Just push *play* on the video, and then reference this handbook.

THE METHOD

We believe in providing you with a full-scale game plan for growth. We are not just giving you content, but a *method* that has been field-tested with hundreds of thousands. While choosing the material is essential, we believe our step-by-step process is one of the best for producing a spiritual change. We have tested the components in each session and how they link together within a series or group of series that complement ongoing growth. Our goal is to produce life change. In each lesson, you will notice clear goals and outcomes, purposeful reflection and discussion questions, a rich study of God's Word, and practical application with actionable steps to be taken. While we know you need content, we hope our commitment to this method deepens their relationship with Christ and with one another.

THERE IS MORE

Remember, once you finish this series there are many others that follow it and build upon it. Don't do just one series, do them all!

HOW TO LEAD A GROUP

ONE | GATHER YOUR TEAM

Assembling a team is critical. A team should include a pair of leaders who become the *"On-Site Hosts"* for the experience. We believe working in pairs is by far the most practical approach. Remember, every pilot needs a wingman.

TWO | RECRUIT PARTICIPANTS

Don't stress: whether you recruit half a dozen or a hundred, the content will be useful. We have found the best recruiting success comes from finding people who are hungry to grow spiritually. While the content is suitable for any believer of any age, the best recruit is the one who wants to be there, someone who hungers for the Word of God, and occasionally some food as well!

THREE | MAKE SURE EACH PARTICIPANT HAS A HANDBOOK

Our guides may be purchased in the online store: www.beresolute.org. These are your guides for taking notes, guiding a dialogue in your group, and recording outcomes at the end of every lesson. Handbooks also include other materials for additional development. You will want one for each lesson series.

FOUR | ONLINE RESOURCES FOR LEADERS

If you have purchased online video access with your membership, you can view all the material. You will be able to listen to audio recaps, watch the videos, read the full transcripts, and even review past lessons. There are also training articles and videos online to help you lead your group.

FIVE | MORE MATERIAL & VINCE MILLER

At Resolute, we are not just providing content. We are inviting you to an experience. Here are other tools you can utilize.

- Need a devotional? Read the Daily Devotional: www. beresolute.org/mdd
- Need prayer? Vince Miller will personally pray for you: www.beresolute.org
- Need a speaker? Invite Vince Miller to speak: beresolute.org/vince-miller
- Need help as a leader? Contact Vince Miller directly at vince@beresolute.org

It is our goal to partner with you and your ministry. We want to resource you with tools that compliment your development as a follower and a leader.

SIX | CONNECT SOCIALLY

We would love to have you join our social networks. Head to our home page and connect with us on Twitter, LinkedIn, and Facebook.

ABOUT VINCE MILLER

Vince Miller was born in Vallejo, California. At twenty, he made a profession of faith while in college and felt a strong, sudden call to work in full-time ministry. After college and graduate school, he invested two decades working with notable ministries like Young Life, InterVarsity Christian Fellowship, and in senior leadership within the local church. He currently resides in St. Paul, Minnesota, with his wife, Christina. They have three adult children.

Then in March 2014, he founded Resolute out of his passion for discipleship and leadership development of men. This passion was born out of his personal need for growth. Vince turned everywhere to find a man who would mentor, disciple, and develop him throughout his spiritual life. He often received two answers from well-meaning Christian leaders: *either they did not know what to do in a mentoring relationship, or they did not have the time to do it.* Vince learned that he was not alone. Many Christian men were seeking this type of mentorship relationship. Therefore, he felt compelled to build an organization that would focus on two things: ensuring that men who want to be discipled have the opportunity and that they have real tools to disciple other men.

Vince is an authentic and transparent leader who loves to communicate with men and has a deep passion for God's Word. He has authored several dozen books, and he is the primary content creator of all Resolute content and discipleship materials.

Keep moving forward,

AN INTRODUCTION TO DANIEL

Daniel is a fascinating man with a fascinating story. His story begins as a teenager. He's taken into captivity, castrated, reeducated, and renamed. He lives in exile in Babylon under multiple kings, but one in particular: Nebuchadnezzar. King Nebuchadnezzar is the greatest potentate ever to exist. He ruled the known world. For this study, we are going to read the account of these two men. It's compelling. And in the end, we are going to learn how to suffer under an enemy king, in a foreign land, under woke ideologies, with strange gods, against jealous plots, under powerful rulers, and still remain faithful.

The question I have for you as we begin is: *Are you that man?*

Or maybe the better question is: *Do you want to be that man?*

If so, you are reading the right book of the Bible, because Daniel is the man to show us the way.

TRUTH FOR RADICAL TIMES

OPENING QUESTIONS

- What cultural changes have presented challenges for God's man?
- Where are these challenges happening the most for you (world, family, work, or church)?
- What things should godly men be doing in these times?
- What things should godly men not be doing in these times?

SESSION ONE

We live in times where the cultural landscape is radically changing; it is unsettling for many Christian men. And while you think such change is new, it's not. It's only new to you. The things we are experiencing right now in our culture have been faced by God's men many times before. The book of Daniel is a chronicle of these events and how one man remained faithful during radical cultural change.

There are three characters we are immediately introduced to in verse one.

First, there is Jehoiakim, the 18th king of Judah. He was not appointed by God but by the Egyptian Pharoah, who, in a roundabout way, controlled Judah at the time. Jehoiakim was 25 when he became ruler and ruled for 11 years. He is described by the biblical authors as a horrible king. He had sex with his mother, daughter-in-law, and stepmother. He murdered men, raped their wives, and stole their property. He performed an epispasm (which means he had his circumcision reversed) to conceal that he was a Jew. And finally, he tattooed his body, which was prohibited by his religious law.

Second, we have Nebuchadnezzar. Historically this was actually Nebuchadnezzar II, also known as Nebuchadnezzar the Great. He ruled Babylon for 43 years, and during his time the Babylonian empire became a world superpower. He kept taking land and constructing buildings when Egypt, Israel, and other powers were in decline. The city of Babylon (the capital of the Babylonian Empire) was massive and glorious. This is where the book of Daniel begins: Israel has fallen, and God's people are taken captive to Babylon.

Third, there is Daniel. This book is a story about his life. Daniel is a teenager when he is taken and becomes a refugee in Babylon. For the 12 chapters of his book, we get an overview of his life and prophecies. What I love about this book is that he's going to be faithful from beginning to end, all 70 years of his captive life.

So we have three notable men. An unfaithful king. An enemy king. A man who worships the only King.

All this begins in Daniel 1:1-2 with a takeover. Here is how the first verses read:

In the third year of the reign of Jehoiakim king of Judah, Nebuchadnezzar king of Babylon came to Jerusalem and besieged it. And the Lord gave Jehoiakim king of Judah into his hand, with some of the vessels of the house of God.

— DANIEL 1:1-2

In the first two verses, we are confronted with a monumental event on the timeline of Israel. God's people are taken over by Babylon. At least, it looks like a takeover. Then as you read the text slowly again, you'll see Daniel states, *"And the Lord gave Jehoiakim king of Judah into his hand."* which results in an obvious question:

Why did God give his land and people over to be enslaved by an enemy superpower? We must keep in mind that there is a lot of history that landed Israel in this predicament before these first two verses were written. Israel had been persistently disobedient for many years and had refused to listen to God. God even gave them a fair warning to repent, or they would reap his justice.

About 100 years before this event, Isaiah the prophet declared:

> *Behold, the days are coming, when all that is in your*
> *house, and that which your fathers have stored up till this*
> *day, shall be carried to Babylon. Nothing shall be left, says*
> *the Lord. And some of your own sons, who will come from*
> *you, whom you will father, shall be taken away, and they*
> *shall be eunuchs in the palace of the king of Babylon.*
>
> **— ISAIAH 39:6-7**

I would say 100 years is a pretty fair warning from God. But Israel chose not to take God seriously.

Frequently mankind doesn't take God seriously enough. We intentionally distance ourselves from God because we want to do the things *we* want to do. As a result, we begin this slow fade from God. Gradually we look more and more like men of the culture than the men of God. When we choose this path, God gives us over to the world, and what we want to do is imitate the desires and actions of the world. Many are caught off-guard by it because it happens so slowly over a long period of time. Then, when God shows up to bring justice, we don't like it.

In the shadow of this moment, Daniel is going to show us how to live as God's man in a time of radical cultural change. We will learn from Daniel how to live godly even when we are under persecution—not just from one king but numerous enemy kings over 70 years—and, thus, how we can remain faithful even as we experience the same difficulties as Daniel.

So, if you have been looking for how to be faithful during oppressive times, Daniel is the book, and Daniel is the man. He is going to show us how.

In the first seven verses of the first chapter we discover three truths for God's man in radical times:

TRUTH ONE | GOD IS WORKING

And he brought them to the land of Shinar, to the house of his god, and placed the vessels in the treasury of his god.

— **DANIEL 1:2B**

Did you notice the beginning of this text? Daniel starts his story with the phrase, *"And he."* The question is, who is the *"he"* doing the bringing here? The *"he"* is God. As we already noted, God was doing the giving of Israel to Babylon, and here he is also doing the bringing. It was God who was giving and bringing Jehoiakim, Jerusalem, the vessels, and the people over to an enemy king. Daniel does not see this moment as a takeover. It's a give-over. He knows that God is working, but God is going to do a different kind of work.

Now, Nebuchadnezzar may have felt like had done it, but Daniel didn't feel this way, nor did he retell the story this way.

23

Do you know why? He was a redeemed man who lived his life directed by a biblical worldview and knew that God is always behind everything. Daniel was entirely good with this situation exactly as God has determined it.

Did you catch where God brought them? *"Shinar."* Do you know where this is? It's an infamous Old Testament location. You can read about it in Genesis 11. It's the location of the Tower of Babel. Now think about this for a minute: God takes his people from the glory of the Temple of God into captivity in the city of the Tower of Babel. A city with walls were 85 feet thick, 300 feet tall, and 60 miles around, protected by a giant moat. Behind these walls, God's people would be enslaved for the next 70 years.

Given the times we live and the changes in culture, don't you wonder how long it might be until God gives us over to our enemies? I do!

Yet, in this change of circumstance, we learn two things from Daniel. First, God is always working, regardless of the challenges we face. Second, God wants to work through faithful men, regardless of our situation.

God will sometimes present us with circumstances we don't like—or a change of circumstance. Like Daniel, we need to see God's sovereignty in the change. Don't confuse this with merely being positive about a bad situation (because this isn't the best of situations). Daniel is going to choose to see the divine reality behind it and embrace it as God has ordered it. Daniel knows

God is at work. And because Daniel understands that God is at work, he does not get in the way of what God is doing. Through the changes, Daniel has not stopped being faithful just because his circumstance has changed.

I think a lot of great men get ensnared by this one. They either think God is not working or that they need to do something to get God working. But all that is needed is faith and obedience. Faith that believes God is still working even when we don't see him. Obedience that acts as if God is still working when we don't see him. Through faith and obedience, we will stay out of God's way so he can do the things he needs to do, and we will join him when the time is right. Otherwise, we might end up just getting in his way by trying to do it our way. That's truth one: remember that God is always working, even when he's not working the way you want.

TRUTH TWO | WE MUST INTIMATELY KNOW GOD'S TRUTH

Then the king commanded Ashpenaz, his chief eunuch, to bring some of the people of Israel, both of the royal family and of the nobility, youths without blemish, of good appearance and skillful in all wisdom, endowed with knowledge, understanding learning, and competent to stand in the king's palace, and to teach them the literature and language of the Chaldeans. The king assigned them a daily portion of the food that

the king ate, and of the wine that he drank. They were to
be educated for three years, and at the end of that time
they were to stand before the king.

— DANIEL 1:3-5

Now we meet Ashpenaz. He is the lead official of the royal household. There are two things we learn about him. First, he is a eunuch, which means he has been castrated. Second, he is tasked with choosing the best and brightest of Israel to bring to Babylon. Notice the list of pre-qualifiers for selecting young men:

- *Without deformity.*
- *Handsome.*
- *Intelligent, well-trained, and quick to learn.*

Basically, Nebuchadnezzar wants the best and brightest. But notice what they do next: they indoctrinate them. He is going to reeducate Israel's best and brightest. Over a three-year period, he will give them the "royal privilege" of learning about Babylonian history, culture, and practices in hopes that they might turn them into sympathizers. This is not free education. It's indoctrination by force where they cannot critically challenge the king and his generosity or education. Nebuchadnezzar's plan is to assimilate captives in hopes of persuading the rest of Israel.

This is happening in our time, just as it did in their day. There are always powerful entities that control the narrative, and by design, they attempt to indoctrinate. Let's not pull punches here. There are political powers, governments, educational systems, social enterprises, large corporations, and media companies that use their platforms to press their narratives. They do it and become more emboldened. They go after the young and teachable, just like Nebuchadnezzar did here.

As we will see more through this book, Daniel knows the truth. He has hidden God's way in his heart. But this is because he's been exposed to it. He has read the scriptures, memorized them, talked about them, and committed to living by them. He knows the truth intimately. Daniel also understands that the Babylonians are not going to allow him to bring his godly culture with him. The only place it lives with him is in his heart, for 70 years.

And that's our duty in our time. We need to know the truth and help others know the truth of God's word. We need to stay close to it, memorize it, and live by every word of it. We should read it in our homes, teach it to our families, and bring it with us into our lives. We should share it and talk about it. God's Word is the only stable and unchanging truth. If we get in it and stay in it, we will discover that indoctrination and propaganda will not have the same effect on us. When the indoctrination and propaganda increase, it will stabilize us, and we will navigate our way through. It's the only book with any truth in it, anyway.

As the writer of Hebrews states:

For the word of God is living and active, sharper than
any two-edged sword, piercing to the division of soul
and of spirit, of joints and of marrow, and discerning the
thoughts and intentions of the heart.

— HEBREWS 4:12

Truth two: We must intimately know God's truth.

TRUTH THREE | GOD WILL NOT & CANNOT BE REMOVED

Among these were Daniel, Hananiah, Mishael,
and Azariah of the tribe of Judah. And the chief of
the eunuchs gave them names: Daniel he called
Belteshazzar, Hananiah he called Shadrach, Mishael he
called Meshach, and Azariah he called Abednego.

— DANIEL 1:6-7

After these young men are marched into captivity into this illustrious city, the first thing the Babylonians do is rename them. But let's quickly note their given names and meaning, and then their Babylonian names and those meanings.

Daniel's name means *God is my judge.*

He is renamed Belteshazzar, which means *Bel protects his life.*

Hananiah's name means *God has acted graciously*.
He is renamed Shadrach, which means *Aku commands*.

Mishael's name means *There is no god like God*.
He is renamed Meshach, which means *Aku is who god is*.

Azariah's name means *God has helped*.
He is renamed Abednego, which means *Nebo is god*.

Hopefully, you see what they are doing. They are not only renaming these young men after Babylonian gods but methodically removing God's name. They are removing any hint of God's name from their identity and language. They are being given new names and definitions based on Babylonian gods. This is the first move of indoctrination: the complete removal of the name of God.

You know, to give someone a name is a powerful thing to do. If you turn back to the beginning of the Bible, you'll see that God spoke, and things came to be. God created light, solar systems, earth, creatures, and mankind by speaking it into existence. He created and gave definitions with words that came from his mouth. By naming, God imparts identity and image to mankind. We see he gave man the power to do the same. He gave him the freedom within the created order to name the creatures of the earth and even woman, whom he named *"Eve — the mother of all the living."* God's people never took the naming of their children lightly. Each one of these four young men had names that identified them as children of God.

In our time, it seems that we want this power for ourselves. We crave the power and control to reidentify ourselves and others. It is no different from what Nebuchadnezzar did. We want to remove God from our culture and assign our own identity, gender, and titles. What is happening in our time is just another manifestation of our futile attempt to play god. But it's a futile attempt.

You can change the calendar from AD to read *Common Era* (C.E.), yet we all know that Jesus is at the center of every date on the modern calendar. You can remove prayer from schools, yet we all know it's to God we turn in times of tragedy in a school, in government, or on a sporting field. You can remove *"in God we trust"* from our currency, yet we all know it's only God who can be trusted and only he who has any value. The reason this is futile is that removing God's name never removes God. If God is God, then he can't be stopped. And that's what we are going to discover through Daniel: enemy superpowers are no match for God, who is seeking men of faith that will be obedient to him even in unfaithful times. He is looking for men like Daniel, Hananiah, Mishael, and Azariah who be faithful in radical cultural change.

Truth three: the one true God will not and cannot be removed.

In only seven verses of chapter one, Daniel has given us everything I think we need to know about being faithful in unfaithful times. Men who are committed to these truths and live by them are the men who see and do incredible things with God. We need more men like this today.

So, are you that man?

REFLECTION & DISCUSSION QUESTIONS

- Which of the three truths most stood out to you? Why?
- How did this truth convict you, and what do you need to do differently?
- What steps are you going to take today and over this week?
- Is there something others can do to help?

PRACTICES OF RESOLUTE MEN

OPENING QUESTIONS

- Do you believe we need more resolute men today? Why?
- List some practices of resolute men. What kinds of things do they do well?
- What do you need to do to become more resolute as a man of God?

SESSION TWO

Imagine this for a moment: you are hundreds of miles from home. You are in a city filled with people who have a very loose moral compass. No one is around keeping a watchful eye on you. You can basically do whatever you want. What do you do?

This is exactly the moment Daniel is thrust into. He is 900 miles from home. He's a young, good-looking, and educated savvy man in a foreign land. Yet we never find one moment of compromise. He is tested to the core and is resolute every single time.

So how about you? How do you respond when no one is looking? Well, don't worry, because you are going to see how to do it the right way. The resolute way.

Here are three practices of resolute men:

PRACTICE ONE | THEY DO NOT COMPROMISE

But Daniel resolved that he would not defile himself with the king's food, or with the wine that he drank. Therefore he asked the chief of the eunuchs to allow him not to defile himself. And God gave Daniel favor and compassion in the sight of the chief of the eunuchs.

— DANIEL 1:8-9

Daniel is moments into enemy captivity. He is being given the royal treatment. Honestly, it's lavish. He's in a metropolitan city that's very advanced. He has a great living situation. He is being trained by the best teachers. He is given the best food, or so it would seem.

The first challenge Daniel encounters is what's on the menu. The food and drink are fit for the king, but Daniel has a two-fold issue with the meal plan. First, great portions of the meat served in the Babylonian palace (*e.g.*, pork and venison) were from unclean animals according to his religious laws. Second, all food and drink were first offered sacrificially to Babylonian gods. This means eating their food was understood as the indirect worship of those gods, which again was also forbidden by his religious law. So, in his first days, Daniel is faced with a real predicament. He can choose to cower in captivity, or he can choose to challenge his captors courageously. As we see, he chooses the latter. He chooses to challenge courageously.

We face predicaments like this all the time. Situations that put pressure on us to compromise our biblical beliefs, values, and convictions. Maybe it's the pressure of a company, the agenda of a leader, or the pressure of peers whose values oppose the values of our faith. Or it could be a situation where we find we are alone in a compromising position where we are free to act contrary to our beliefs. Or we might feel relational pressure not to act on godly convictions because it might put another person in a real predicament. I think Daniel weighed all these choices. He felt the pressure of an influential leader, the freedom of compromising a situation, and the pressure not to act in a way that might put his friends at risk. But Daniel still made a resolute choice. I believe he made this choice because he decided in his mind that it was better to endure the justice of God than the injustice of anyone else.

How about you? What would you have done? Be honest, because for Daniel this was a real situation and a real predicament.

Speaking for myself, I can only say with confidence today that I know I would not compromise—but I am not sure I would have done that when I was a teenage boy in a foreign land, imprisoned under an enemy king right after I had been imprisoned by the most powerful man in the world at the time. It has taken me years to learn that the more my faith and trust in God grows, the less willing I am to make these compromises. As I have grown spiritually in my relationship with God and become more familiar with what he wants for me and from me, I have greatly reduced my willingness to compromise. Today, even within the confines of my private thoughts, I have trouble making compromises because I know God knows even the intention of my heart. This means I am trying more today to deal with compromise on the level of intentions before it leads to compromising behavior. The only way to become a man who is unwilling to compromise is to be fully aligned with a God who never compromises.

If you want to be a more resolute man, then you have to practice uncompromising behavior. You must choose not to test the line and boundaries of disobedience. You must choose to bring your intentions to God, and not just your behaviors. If you learn to let God deal with your bad intentions, you'll discover that one decision at a time you'll make fewer compromises, and you won't put yourself in compromising situations. Maybe one day you'll meet a test as Daniel did. One where you have to choose, "do I compromise a meal so I don't piss off a king or my friends?" You'll meet it with a confidence that declares:

"I would rather live an uncompromised life with God, than live a compromised life without him."

Practice one: They do not compromise.

PRACTICE TWO | THEY ACT ON GODLY CONVICTIONS

...and the chief of the eunuchs said to Daniel, "I fear my lord the king, who assigned your food and your drink; for why should he see that you were in worse condition than the youths who are of your own age? So you would endanger my head with the king." Then Daniel said to the steward whom the chief of the eunuchs had assigned over Daniel, Hananiah, Mishael, and Azariah, "Test your servants for ten days; let us be given vegetables to eat and water to drink. Then let our appearance and the appearance of the youths who eat the king's food be observed by you, and deal with your servants according to what you see." So he listened to them in this matter, and tested them for ten days. At the end of ten days it was seen that they were better in appearance and fatter in flesh than all the youths who ate the king's food. So the steward took away their food and the wine they were to drink, and gave them vegetables.

— DANIEL 1:10-16

Daniel just made a choice not to compromise. But now he must act, and how he approaches the challenge will shape the outcome of his conviction.

I believe godly men always feel these spiritual convictions. I know this is the case because the Spirit is always convicting. That's his job. But our response to this conviction makes all the difference. There are two extreme responses. The first extreme is the man who acts on the conviction quickly, but his overly passionate approach leaves devastation in his path. Thus, he and others suffer. The second extreme is the man who hesitates to act on the conviction, and his passivity leaves destruction in his path. Thus, he and others suffer. I have seen both extremes. Let's be honest, we have done both. You and I have been on both ends of these extremes. We have done both at home, work, school, and church, and they result in problems that don't play out very well. Our attempt at becoming resolute men is foiled because of our passion or hesitation.

But Daniel gives us the ultimate model. He demonstrates how resolute men approach a challenge. He is convicted and determined. A step must be taken promptly; otherwise, passivity will set in. At the same time, his actions cannot be overly passionate, or he will endanger himself and others. So here is what he does: he is respectful, tactful, and presents a solution. Let's unpack these three.

First, **he is respectful** by speaking to his superior about his conviction because he knows his conviction could be interpreted as disrespectful. To reject a provision of the king was to reject the king. So Daniel, while passionate, must regulate his passion. I think a lot of men forget this. We believe our passion gives us the right to interject our beliefs disrespectfully, but it doesn't. It is possible to take a hard stand without being hard on people, with the hope of winning them over.

Second, **he is tactful** and speaks up about his conviction. He's not going to be passive. He must verbalize his beliefs. He makes them known, not just to his three friends, but to the person who has the power to make the needed change. He presents them diplomatically. He takes a stand but speaks in a way Ashpenaz will listen. So for you guys who tend toward passivity or passion, be tactful.

Third, **he presents a solution**. Daniel is in a predicament, but he also knows this will present a dilemma for his superior. So instead of just presenting a problem, he offers a solution, a substitute meal plan. And, of course, it works. This is another thing we can do, present a real solution to the challenge we're facing.

What we get at the end is an incredible example. A resolute man who approaches challenges resolutely by being respectful, tactful, and solution-oriented. And guess what? Everyone wins in this situation. Daniel. Ashpenaz. Nebuchadnezzar. Even the three friends. Now, this is not guaranteed to work exactly like this every time. There are plenty of times resolute men in the Bible approached a challenge and were stoned, flogged, crucified, or beheaded. I can think of a few examples. But why not first try what Daniel did right here? Be respectful. Be tactful. Be solution-oriented.

Practice two: Act on godly conviction.

PRACTICE THREE | THEY IMPACT MORE THAN THEY'RE IMPACTED

As for these four youths, God gave them learning and skill in all literature and wisdom, and Daniel had understanding in all visions and dreams. At the end of the time, when the king had commanded that they should be brought in, the chief of the eunuchs brought them in before Nebuchadnezzar. And the king spoke with them, and among all of them none was found like Daniel, Hananiah, Mishael, and Azariah. Therefore they stood before the king. And in every matter of wisdom and understanding about which the king inquired of them, he found them ten times better than all the magicians and enchanters that were in all his kingdom.

— **DANIEL 1:17-20**

Resolute men understand that every decision has potential for greatly impacting others. Sometimes these decisions can have a strong negative or positive impact that put others in a real bind. For example, Daniel's decision to take the moral high ground with the menu put three groups of people in jeopardy. First, it put the power structure over him in a real pickle. His superiors, like the chief eunuch and the servant, were at real risk of losing their heads for making a unilateral adjustment for them. Second, it also put the three friends in a bind. By association Hananiah, Mishael, and Azariah were culpable by association. Third, don't forget that Daniel's decision also put the other Israelite captives at risk, too. Remember, there had been many Israelites who did not take the same moral stand because they did not take the risk. Depending on how the whole situation pans out, there could have been an impact on them as well.

Being a resolute man means we assess the risks, weigh them against practice one and two above, and then act with confidence. Here's why. Every decision and non-decision a man makes impacts others. If Daniel acts, or does not, it's going to impact all three groups. But the resolute man acts in obedience to God's truth and allows obedience and faith to have an impact. Then we must trust the outcomes to God. That's how faith works. Choosing obedience and leaving the outcome to God requires faith. Choosing intentional disobedience does not. Yet here's the deal, both decisions impact others.

Practice three: Resolute men impact others more than they are impacted by them.

If you want to grow in this area, the decisions are relatively simple: do what Daniel did. Make fewer compromises, act on those godly convictions, and start having an impact rather than being impacted by others. The best thing you could do today to start the process is choose one of the three practices that need improvement, determine why you need to improve and take a small step today. In fact, the questions below will help.

REFLECTION & DISCUSSION QUESTIONS

- Which one of the three practices needs improvement in your journey of becoming a resolute man?
- Why is this?
- What practical step can you take today?
- How can you repeat this step every day this week?
- What resistance do you expect to encounter?
- How will you respond?

HOW TO STAND UP FOR GOD

OPENING QUESTIONS

- What does it look like when a man "stands up for God?"
- Is there a wrong way to stand up for God?
- Who is someone you know that does it well? Describe how they do it.

SESSION THREE

Many men today believe that they cannot make a difference in the world today. And they are right. They cannot. At least not by their own power and might. But a man indwelled by the Spirit of God can make a huge difference in the world. God's man can and will see and do incredible things. If you want to do and see these things, then you need to get some things right.

In a quick reading of Daniel chapter two, we will see that one godly man can accomplish impossible things. What happens is that God penetrates the palace and the mind of king Nebuchadnezzar with a disturbing dream. Then he demands

DANIEL

that someone tell him the undisclosed dream and interpret it, which everyone believes is an impossible task. But then a man stands up: Daniel. An enslaved Israelite held captive is going to reveal the undisclosed dream and also reveal its meaning. Hope and salvation come from God through one man who chose to stand up. But he had to stand up to the greatest world leader of all time, King Nebuchadnezzar.

Today I hope you will discover that you, as God's man, can have this same effect on the world. Even when the odds look impossible, God in and through you can make a difference. But here's the deal you are going to have to take a stand. But as you do, you need to do it the right way, and Daniel is going to show us how.

Here are four actions for the man who aspires to take a stand for God.

ACTION ONE | STAND ON SPIRITUAL CONFIDENCE

Therefore Daniel went in to Arioch, whom the king had appointed to destroy the wise men of Babylon. He went and said thus to him: "Do not destroy the wise men of Babylon; bring me in before the king, and I will show the king the interpretation."

— DANIEL 2:24

44

So here enters Daniel. At the last second Daniel walks in and declares, *"Stop what you're doing. Don't kill all the seers and magicians. Take me to the king. I will explain the dream."*

Don't you love this *"take me to the king"* moment?

But don't be confused about Daniel's confidence. This is not self-confidence; it's confidence in God. Daniel has no awareness of the situation or the details, but he knows God can provide a solution, so he stands up. I think sometimes God-fearing men misunderstand and misappropriate this.

As God's men, the more time we spend in scripture, the more our minds will adjust to a biblical worldview. With this mindset, we begin to see things more clearly, and as we do, we will develop more confidence. But this presents a unique challenge for the man who follows God. The danger is in assuming that the wisdom we have gained is something we can use for personal advantage. It's not. If we do this, spiritual confidence will become self-confidence, which is just another manifestation of self-righteousness, and that's a move against God.

So while Daniel has this *"take me to the king"* confidence, don't interpret this as self-confidence. It's not confidence based on his ability, but rather a faith that God will provide the ability and knowledge when the time is right. I know this is true based on what happens next. Listen to the following few verses:

Then Arioch brought in Daniel before the king in haste and said thus to him: "I have found among the exiles from Judah a man who will make known to the king the interpretation." The king declared to Daniel, whose name was Belteshazzar, "Are you able to make known to me the dream that I have seen and its interpretation?" Daniel answered the king and said, "No wise men, enchanters, magicians, or astrologers can show to the king the mystery that the king has asked, but there is a God in heaven who reveals mysteries, and he has made known to King Nebuchadnezzar what will be in the latter days. Your dream and the visions of your head as you lay in bed are these: To you, O king, as you lay in bed came thoughts of what would be after this, and he who reveals mysteries made known to you what is to be. But as for me, this mystery has been revealed to me, not because of any wisdom that I have more than all the living, but in order that the interpretation may be made known to the king, and that you may know the thoughts of your mind.

— DANIEL 2:25-30

Did you hear that? He clarifies that *"no wise men, enchanters, magicians, or astrologers"* can reveal the mystery, *"but there's a God in heaven who can."* He is careful to clarify that it's not him. He is there by faith alone. Then later, he adds, *"this mystery has been revealed to me, not because of any wisdom that I have."*

While Daniel is 100% confident, it's 100% confidence in God. He knows that the insight and wisdom are not his to possess.

He is a mere steward who is confident in God. What's so ironic about this moment is that Nebuchadnezzar had God's name intentionally removed from his name. But God takes some remarkable steps to make his name known to him.

We need men like this in our time. Men who will stand up with 100% confidence in God, and nothing else. They only want to give glory, attention, and credit to God because they want someone else to believe in him.

Now it's your turn. What do you need to do to stand in spiritual confidence?

ACTION TWO | STAND AGAINST THE RIGHT OPPOSITION

This was the dream. Now we will tell the king its interpretation. You, O king, the king of kings, to whom the God of heaven has given the kingdom, the power, and the might, and the glory, and into whose hand he has given, wherever they dwell, the children of man, the beasts of the field, and the birds of the heavens, making you rule over them all—you are the head of gold.

— DANIEL 2:36-38

At this point, Daniel tells king Nebuchadnezzar about his dream through supernatural revelation. Keep in mind that the king is probably a little shocked, especially given the detail with which

Daniel describes his untold dream. But right into this drama, Daniel inserts a vital reminder. The reminder is this:

"You might be the current reigning emperor of the world, but the God who gave you this dream, and gave me the ability to tell you this dream, is the God who has done this. He is the God who created the world, distributes power, determines rulers, conveys dreams, and interprets dreams."

This is the kind of man God wants to use, the one who is unafraid of standing before spiritual opposition. Nebuchadnezzar is no ordinary king. He is a pagan. He is the greatest reigning superpower on the planet, and an enemy of God. He has overpowered God's nation and taken Israel into captivity. Yet we see that Daniel isn't vindictive, angry, or on attack when he gets his first opportunity to appear before the king. He doesn't curse or insult him. Daniel can act this way because he knows that God is behind at the events, not Nebuchadnezzar.

I think sometimes believers misunderstand what it means for us to stand against our opposition. We are called to stand against all *spiritual* opposition. Yet, at the same time, as we do it, we must be careful not to stand in the way of God. Daniel models how to do this. Nebuchadnezzar is his spiritual opposition. But Daniel knows something. He knows that God brought the nation into exile because of their unfaithfulness. So, Daniel is content to trust God in this circumstance. Should Daniel compromise his beliefs because his circumstances changed? No. But Daniel must find new ways to stand against his opposition. As God's man, he must be careful not to take matters into his own hands as he stands up for his beliefs. He had to be careful that in the process of standing against the king, he didn't end up standing against God.

Daniel also knows God has given him a spiritual gift with extraordinary power, but Daniel must steward this in a way that brings attention to God, not himself or even his sense of justice. Notably, he speaks into this moment, reminding Nebuchadnezzar that he might be great, but there is a greater King.

Fellas, it is good to remind ourselves that God is always in charge. It may not seem like it, but he's got this. If (or when) God calls you to stand against spiritual opposition, go for it and speak up. But as you do it, be careful not to stand in God's way because no man, not us or our enemies, stands against the greatness of our God.

Now it's your turn. Like Daniel, you are called to stand for righteousness in your workplace or community, but like Daniel you are called to demonstrate respect toward those in authority—not because they are always right, but because God placed them those positions. Your stand for righteousness has more power when you avoid vindictive and angry words. What do you need to do to stand against the right opposition and do it the right way?

ACTION THREE | TRUST IN GOD'S WORD

Another kingdom inferior to you shall arise after you, and yet a third kingdom of bronze, which shall rule over all the earth. And there shall be a fourth kingdom, strong as iron, because iron breaks to pieces and shatters all things. And like iron that crushes, it shall break and crush all these. And as you saw the feet and toes, partly of potter's clay and partly of iron, it shall be a divided kingdom, but some of the firmness of iron shall be in it, just as you saw iron mixed with the soft clay. And as the toes of the feet were partly iron and partly clay, so the kingdom shall be partly strong and partly brittle. As you saw the iron mixed with soft clay, so they will mix with one another in marriage, but they will not hold together, just as iron does not mix with clay. And in the days of those kings the God of heaven will set up a kingdom that shall never be destroyed, nor shall the kingdom be left to another people. It shall break in pieces all these kingdoms and bring them to an end, and it shall stand forever, just as you saw that a stone was cut from a mountain by no human hand, and that it broke in pieces the iron, the bronze, the clay, the silver, and the gold. A great God has made known to the king what shall be after this. The dream is certain, and its interpretation sure.

— DANIEL 2:39-45

This is an incredible dream and revelation. It makes known centuries of future events. No wonder the king was terrified by it. He was given a glimpse far into the future. And get this: Nebuchadnezzar was not a God-fearing man. I think it's laughable because we have a lot of self-declared God-fearing men out there today who claim to know biblical events in the future, and yet God gave it to someone who did not know or fear him. I believe God does so in order that we will know the expanse of his power and revelation.

Daniel tells the king that his untold dream speaks of four great world empires. While Daniel and Nebuchadnezzar knew them to be world empires, they did not know whom the four empires represented. Today, we do. First is the Babylonian empire, which represents the head of gold. Second is the Medo-Persian empire, which represents the silver chest and arms. The third is the Greek empire which represents the bronze belly and thighs. And fourth is the Roman Empire which represents the iron legs. We understand this because we can look back over hundreds of years with a greater perspective.

Two things grab my attention about this dream. First is the perspective that Nebuchadnezzar has of this image. He pictures himself standing before it and is amazed and frightened by its size, sparkle, and craftsmanship. Second, the king then witnesses a huge stone hurled with such great force at the image that it annihilates him. Did you note the detail of the stone? It's a stone that was not crafted or launched by human hands. It was crafted by someone greater and more powerful than what created the image. This terrified the king.

In many ways, this dream still terrifies us. There are things about this prophecy we understand today only because history has revealed them. Yet there are some bits and pieces of it that we still do not understand. But this is just like our God. He gives us just enough detail that we'll know what's happening when it's happening but not so much that it exonerates us from trusting him by faith.

For example, did you know there are about 20-25 books in our world today that claim to be a form of divine revelation? Only 20-25 books claim to have some form of divine revelation by a spiritual leader. Yet, in all these books, except for the Holy Bible, there is one thing missing: detailed prophecy. Detailed prophecies presenting enough compound improbability that would make it only possible to be known and disclosed by the one true God. Right here in Daniel chapter two, that's what we have. Centuries of prophecy in such profound detail that only God could accurately predict them. Some of these kingdoms did not even exist at the time. God proves once again that only he knows the end game and that the seers and prophets of their day were no match for the God of all Gods.

This prophecy opposes the power, wisdom, and expanse of Nebuchadnezzar's power. It's a prophecy that is so incredible that it's going to outlast him, and he knows it. The king has met his match. He must come to the end of himself. His empire may last a while longer, but the true King is going to outlast him.

This is the nature of God's Word. God's Word will eventually oppose every proud and powerful man. It will stand against them and outlast them. At some point, we must tell them this; otherwise, they are going to be for a brutal awakening too late.

God knows the times in which we live. He knows the leaders of this world are losing their minds. But guess what? He's got it all figured out. His Word tells the story. We must trust that he will use us as his mouthpiece for his Word till his Holy Empire comes again.

Now it's your turn. What do you need to do to trust more in God's Word?

ACTION FOUR | BELIEVE THAT GOD CAN REACH STUBBORN MEN

Then King Nebuchadnezzar fell upon his face and paid homage to Daniel, and commanded that an offering and incense be offered up to him. The king answered and said to Daniel, "Truly, your God is God of gods and Lord of kings, and a revealer of mysteries, for you have been able to reveal this mystery." Then the king gave Daniel high honors and many great gifts, and made him ruler over the whole province of Babylon and chief prefect over all the wise men of Babylon. Daniel made a request of the king, and he appointed Shadrach, Meshach, and Abednego over the affairs of the province of Babylon. But Daniel remained at the king's court.

— DANIEL 2:46-49

Awesome, right?

God took one of the great global monarchs, someone who didn't even believe in the God of Israel, brought him to his knees through a dream, and turned him into a believer, at least at this moment in time.

Notice what Nebuchadnezzar does in this text:

- *He fell to the ground.*
- *He thanked Daniel.*
- *He made an offering.*
- *He declared God the God of gods and revealer of mysteries.*
- *He also showered Daniel with gifts.*
- *He elevated Daniel's role.*
- *He granted Daniel's request.*

Don't be distracted by the offerings, the blessings, the advancement, and the provision of the king to Daniel. That's just temporal stuff. The amazement of this moment is that this very stubborn and self-righteous king has bowed before the work and revelation of God. Daniel is a mere recipient of something God has done. This world leader has been (at least temporarily) humbled by the event of God's revelation.

In my opinion, this moment is one of the great moments in history. God took an arrogant and disobedient man and turned his heart to him. He has done this with countless well-known personalities. Like lead singer Brian Welch from Korn, professional model Nikki Taylor, NASCAR driver Jeff Gordon, and music legends Bob Dylan and Alice Cooper. I believe God still wants to do stuff like this. I think he still can. He is ready to turn antagonistic, enraged, narcissistic men and leaders into believers. Yet there is one critical component we cannot miss from the story: God wants to use his men to do this. He is looking for one faithful, available, and humble man willing to lead the way.

Now it's your turn. Do you believe that God can reach the most stubborn of men?

We have looked at four actions of Daniel as he stood up for God. He was spiritually confident. He stood against the right opposition. He trusted God's Word. He believes that God could change even the most stubborn heart. If you need to stand up for God, then do what Daniel did. When the time comes, keep pointing to God. He deserves all the credit, anyway.

REFLECTION & DISCUSSION QUESTIONS

- Which of the four actions is something you need to address today?
- Why do you need to address this one?
- What small step do you need to take?
- How can another man help?

GODLY REPONSES TO MALICIOUS PEOPLE

OPENING QUESTIONS

- Do you believe malicious things are happening in government, education, business, and the church?
- Why are these things happening?
- What needs to be done about them?
- What would Jesus do if he were here today?

SESSION FOUR

Let's recall where we have been. King Nebuchadnezzar is the king who rules the greatest empire on the planet. He recently overpowered Judah and Jerusalem, taking captive some of the best and brightest of God's people. Then four young men become the center of the story. They are Daniel, Shadrach, Meshach, and Abednego. They walked hundreds of miles to the city of Babylon, which is modern-day Iraq. They were re-educated at a liberal university in Babylon. Then they were physically mutilated by castration, which is slightly further than circumcision but not as far as sexual reassignment. To top it off, they were given new names that delete God's name from their identity. These occurrences are fascinating, given what we see happening in our culture.

Then Nebuchadnezzar has this terrifying dream and demands that someone tells him the dream and the interpretation; otherwise, he will kill all the magicians and seers. And right at the last minute, Daniel comes forward to tell him about the dream and the interpretation. For a second, we witness what appears to be a reverent king. But don't be fooled. We haven't gotten into chapter three yet.

As we begin chapter three, we fast-forward about twenty years. Daniel is in his thirties by this time, and here's what happens next in Babylon:

King Nebuchadnezzar made an image of gold, whose height was sixty cubits and its breadth six cubits. He set it up on the plain of Dura, in the province of Babylon. Then King Nebuchadnezzar sent to gather the satraps, the prefects, and the governors, the counselors, the treasurers, the justices, the magistrates, and all the officials of the provinces to come to the dedication of the image that King Nebuchadnezzar had set up. Then the satraps, the prefects, and the governors, the counselors, the treasurers, the justices, the magistrates, and all the officials of the provinces gathered for the dedication of the image that King Nebuchadnezzar had set up. And they stood before the image that Nebuchadnezzar had set up. And the herald proclaimed aloud, "You

*are commanded, O peoples, nations, and languages,
that when you hear the sound of the horn, pipe, lyre,
trigon, harp, bagpipe, and every kind of music, you are
to fall down and worship the golden image that King
Nebuchadnezzar has set up. And whoever does not
fall down and worship shall immediately be cast into
a burning fiery furnace." Therefore, as soon as all the
peoples heard the sound of the horn, pipe, lyre, trigon,
harp, bagpipe, and every kind of music, all the peoples,
nations, and languages fell down and worshiped the
golden image that King Nebuchadnezzar had set up.*

— **DANIEL 3:1-7**

So Nebuchadnezzar does not have a problem with self-esteem.
But the story continues.

*Therefore at that time certain Chaldeans came forward
and maliciously accused the Jews. They declared to King
Nebuchadnezzar, "O king, live forever! You, O king, have
made a decree, that every man who hears the sound of
the horn, pipe, lyre, trigon, harp, bagpipe, and every kind
of music, shall fall down and worship the golden image.
And whoever does not fall down and worship shall be cast
into a burning fiery furnace. There are certain Jews whom
you have appointed over the affairs of the province of
Babylon: Shadrach, Meshach, and Abednego. These men,
O king, pay no attention to you; they do not serve your
gods or worship the golden image that you have set up."*

— **DANIEL 3:8-12**

We discover a group of jealous people (magicians and seers) are policing the king's mandate here. I think we get what's happening. We have all been victimized by mandates. Or we have been victimized by jealous and malicious people who police them. This does happen just about everywhere if you think about it. It happens between political parties at all levels of government. It happens in schools, churches, and homes between malicious students, members, and siblings. Jealous people will do devious and malicious things. That is what these Chaldeans are doing because they are jealous of the promotion that three God-fearing men got after the interpretation of the king's dream.

This happens when jealousy goes unaddressed for too long. Eventually, an unregulated jealous spirit will desire to control when they feel out of control. This issue has been brewing for at least a decade. So these men have devised a pretty elaborate plan. This group of jealous Chaldeans presents a mandate, the king endorses the mandate, they police the mandate, and then entrap Shadrach, Meshach, and Abednego with the mandate. Their jealousy has not matured into a full-blown scandal that attempts to exert control because they feel out of control.

But while this might get you all worked up, don't forget that all this begins in the human heart. No dictator, monarch, business leader, manager, authority, or parent can mandate enough laws to control how wild and sinful the human heart will be. So, the question is not why does this happen or when is going to happen. The question always is how do we respond to this? How do we respond to people who are intentionally malicious? How can we respond so we don't fall into the same trap?

Here are three godly responses of God's man.

FIRST RESPONSE| BE OBEDIENT ONE STEP AT A TIME

Then Nebuchadnezzar in furious rage commanded that Shadrach, Meshach, and Abednego be brought. So they brought these men before the king. Nebuchadnezzar answered and said to them, "Is it true, O Shadrach, Meshach, and Abednego, that you do not serve my gods or worship the golden image that I have set up? Now if you are ready when you hear the sound of the horn, pipe, lyre, trigon, harp, bagpipe, and every kind of music, to fall down and worship the image that I have made, well and good. But if you do not worship, you shall immediately be cast into a burning fiery furnace. And who is the god who will deliver you out of my hands?" Shadrach, Meshach, and Abednego answered and said to the king, "O Nebuchadnezzar, we have no need to answer you in this matter. If this be so, our God whom we serve is able to deliver us from the burning fiery furnace, and he will deliver us out of your hand, O king. But if not, be it known to you, O king, that we will not serve your gods or worship the golden image that you have set up."

— DANIEL 3:13-18

The king is pretty hacked off at these guys for several reasons. First, they refuse to worship his gods. Second, they refuse to worship him. I think it's safe to say that Nebuchadnezzar has become a full-blown narcissist. He has convinced himself that he is a god and he's worthy of worship. He believes that no one will save these three men from his god-like vengeance. He is completely unaware of the scandal that the Chaldeans have conceived.

But Shadrach, Meshach, and Abednego are going to take a stand for their convictions. They make two declarations to the king. First, that God has more power than him. Second, that worshipping God is more beneficial. It's important to note that they are not putting God to the test. Instead, they are being faithful regardless of the outcome. I don't think they care about the outcome at all. They don't know the outcome. In life or death, they are making the choice go down as three men who were going to be faithful to God in a faithless time.

These are the kind of men God is looking for: all out and all in men. I believe God-fearing men aspire to be men like these guys, but we cannot be like these men if we don't do what they did. These men took daily steps of obedience, not only in one moment of time, but over the last 20 years of their captivity. They took steps of obedience until they were met with the next step, which proved to be the ultimate test. The test of ultimate faith. The opportunity to give their lives for what they declared they believed.

I believe we each face moments like this in our lives. It may not look exactly like this, but on a smaller scale and to some degree, it will feel like this. It could come sooner than you think. But until then, we need to live every day like we trust the power and benefit of God. We must act as if we trust him more than our money, investments, and retirement. That we trust him more than our solutions, power, and abilities. That we trust him more than we do another president, politician, or supreme court ruling. That we trust him more than a specific outcome in our marriage, family, or career. And when that moment comes, you will know exactly what do. It's the same thing these men did. You take the next step of obedience in a long line of steps. But that one step might be the declarative step God uses to reveal his majesty, redeem you, and bring clarity to injustice.

SECOND RESPONSE | DON'T BE SURPRISED AT HEATED OPPOSITION

Then Nebuchadnezzar was filled with fury, and the expression of his face was changed against Shadrach, Meshach, and Abednego. He ordered the furnace heated seven times more than it was usually heated. And he ordered some of the mighty men of his army to bind Shadrach, Meshach, and Abednego, and to cast them into the burning fiery furnace. Then these men were bound in their cloaks, their tunics, their hats, and their other garments, and they were thrown into the burning fiery furnace. Because the king's order was urgent and

*the furnace overheated, the flame of the fire killed those
men who took up Shadrach, Meshach, and Abednego.
And these three men, Shadrach, Meshach, and
Abednego, fell bound into the burning fiery furnace.*

— **DANIEL 3:19-23**

I could be wrong, but I think there's almost no chance you or
I will experience something exactly like this in our lifetime.
Yet we all encounter moments that frighten us to the core.
Moments we are in the hot seat. Moments we feel powerless
and overwhelmed. This could happen on the job, at home, or in
a courtroom. It might be with a person who is a boss, a spouse,
or a leader. But typically, this happens because we've done
something wrong. What we've done comes with a penalty,
lands us in a hot seat, and comes with feelings of regret and
powerlessness.

But these men hadn't sinned. In fact, they refused to sin. They
stood up for God, which required them to stand against a king
who proclaimed to be a god. They chose to do what is right and
righteous and were prepared to suffer for it at the hands of a
cruel, self-righteous, and angry king.

Eventually, God's man will (and should) suffer for doing what
is right and righteous in this life. We should anticipate it and
meet the moment ready to respond. Given the changes in our
culture, it's going to happen more. We cannot back down from
being faithful. With this comes more opportunity for greater

faith in a God who might be taking us to the edge of the flame. Not only to test us but to display his glory through us. For it is only when the flame of persecution is hot, seven times hotter, that we remove all possibility of natural solutions and see the work of a supernatural God who wants to use obedient and faithful men to bring attention to him.

This is what I love about God. He wants us to see incredible and supernatural things. He wants to do these things through us. He will use faithful and obedient men to bring this about so that people will see how incredible God is when he works through his man.

But for this to happen, we've got to be ready to respond and not get caught off guard. So, get ready, fellas. The enemy is turning up the heat.

THIRD RESPONSE | TRIALS WITH GOD PRODUCE THE BEST RESULTS

Then King Nebuchadnezzar was astonished and rose up in haste. He declared to his counselors, "Did we not cast three men bound into the fire?" They answered and said to the king, "True, O king." He answered and said, "But I see four men unbound, walking in the midst of the fire, and they are not hurt; and the appearance of the fourth is like a son of the gods." Then Nebuchadnezzar came near to the door of the burning fiery furnace; he declared, "Shadrach, Meshach, and Abednego, servants

of the Most High God, come out, and come here!" Then
Shadrach, Meshach, and Abednego came out from the
fire. And the satraps, the prefects, the governors, and the
king's counselors gathered together and saw that the
fire had not had any power over the bodies of those men.
The hair of their heads was not singed, their cloaks were
not harmed, and no smell of fire had come upon them.
Nebuchadnezzar answered and said, "Blessed be the
God of Shadrach, Meshach, and Abednego, who has sent
his angel and delivered his servants, who trusted in him,
and set aside the king's command, and yielded up their
bodies rather than serve and worship any god except
their own God. Therefore I make a decree: Any people,
nation, or language that speaks anything against the
God of Shadrach, Meshach, and Abednego shall be torn
limb from limb, and their houses laid in ruins, for there is
no other god who is able to rescue in this way."
Then the king promoted Shadrach, Meshach,
and Abednego in the province of Babylon.

— DANIEL 3:24-30

We live in times ruled by the spirit of Babylon. Malicious men like the Chaldeans and Nebuchadnezzar still exist. They will until the end of this age. This means if you are a believer, you are going to have trouble and opposition in this life. We might even have long seasons of hot trials, trials that are going to test us on a macro level, like those in the world, in our countries, with governments, politicians, and leaders. Trials on a micro level in our marriage, family, workplaces, and personal lives. Somedays, the furnace of these trials is going to rage. Occasionally the heat will get turned way up.

Every man who goes through these trials obediently trusts God has the potential for supernatural outcomes. The operative word here is *potential,* because as well all know, every fiery situation does not turn out exactly as it did for these three men. There were plenty of people in the Bible who suffered fiery torments for standing up for their faith and came out on the other side burned, stoned, beaten, and crucified. But the good news is that we are promised eternal life, which is a supernatural outcome that's guaranteed. If we choose to walk through it obediently and with integrity, we can hold our heads high that while we may not have gotten the natural outcomes we wanted, we did the right thing, and we did it with God. This is the point: we must be willing to trust God regardless of the outcome.

A man of faith always has God by his side. God will stand by him through the fire, even when a vengeful spirit walks him to the edge of the furnace and pushes him in. The man that God experiences something unique that others miss out on. But you'll have to have faith that the Spirit of God is greater than the spirit of this world.

So when you are maliciously attacked by others, be obedient. Don't be surprised. Face the moment with your mighty God by your side.

REFLECTION & DISCUSSION QUESTIONS

- What trial is hot or heating up in your life right now?
- What has been your response to this trial so far?
- Is it because of your sin or the sin of another?
- Is there a motivation that needs to change in your heart?
- How do you need to adjust your response?
- How can others pray for you?

THE JOURNEY MEN TAKE WITH GOD

OPENING QUESTIONS

- What have been a few markers (highs and lows) in your journey with God?
- What have you learned from these moments of God?
- What have you learned about yourself?
- Do you tell this story often? Why or why not?

SESSION FIVE

Chapter four of Daniel is this incredible chronicle of Nebuchadnezzar in his final years with Daniel. It's in this amazing interaction between the two men that we learn so much about who Nebuchadnezzar really is. It captures his spiritual story so well. It looks like an interaction between Nebuchadnezzar and Daniel, but really, it's an interaction with God through Daniel.

This chapter captures the essence of all our stories. It's the progression of one man as he learns about himself, the world, and God. Regardless of whether they believe in God or not, all men are on this same journey. Some of these stories result in a rejection of God, others result in the acceptance of God. Some stories are long, and others are shorter. Some have stories with lots of challenges, and others not so much. But in the end the story centers on God. It is a retelling of events that God had been doing in our lives from the beginning to the present and how he has used certain events to demonstrate his divine power, illuminate the depths of our foolishness, arrogance, and sin, rescue us from our selfishness, and rescue us by his grace, love, mercy, and forgiveness.

As we read about this one man's story, as crazy as it is, I want you to think about your story and where yours connects with his. I hope you realize by the time we are done that you have a story to tell about God as well.

Here are the five parts of Nebuchadnezzar's story:

PART ONE | A FRIGHTENED MAN

I, Nebuchadnezzar, was at ease in my house and prospering in my palace. I saw a dream that made me afraid. As I lay in bed the fancies and the visions of my head alarmed me. So I made a decree that all the wise men of Babylon should be brought before me, that they might make known to me the interpretation of the dream. Then the magicians, the enchanters, the Chaldeans, and the astrologers came in, and I told them the dream, but they could not make known to me its interpretation.

— DANIEL 4:4-7

Nebuchadnezzar has another terrible dream, again. And again, he needs someone to interpret it. This time the process is handled a little differently because the Nebuchadnezzar is going to reveal the details of the dream. This could be for several reasons. Maybe he wants an expedited answer. Maybe because he is more frightened about this dream than the others. Maybe he privately understood the interpretation and wanted clarity. Regardless, he is scared and alarmed. The text tells us of a dramatic and sudden change. In one verse, he's in one state, and in the next, he is a terrified man. And again, it's a dream that causes him to panic.

There is no man alive who is out of God's reach. God can reach the most stubborn, immovable, arrogant, and resistant man. He can get to them inside the confines of their fortress, protected by soldiers, and surrounded by puppets politicians. He can penetrate the mind of mortal man with dreams, visions, images, and nightmares. He can do this anytime and anywhere when he wants to get a man's attention. In the New Testament alone, he did it with military commanders like Cornelius, followers like Ananias, influential religious leaders like Saul, and faithful disciples like Peter. In this case, he reaches into the mind of the world's richest, most powerful, and longest-lasting monarch.

All men are frightened at some point by God. Either it happens during our life or at the end of life, but that moment is coming. The real question at this moment in Nebuchadnezzar's story is *why* he is frightened. Is he afraid because he had a dream? Is his fear driven by the mystery of the unknown meaning in the dream? Is he afraid of knowing the interpretation of the dream? Or is he actually afraid of God, who gave him the dream and told him about his eventual end? We will soon discover that he is not really frightened by God, yet! He has not connected the dots even though Daniel has been trying to help him connect the dots for close to 30 years.

This one detail is a critical part of every man's spiritual story. It's the moment we realize the events of this life are caused not by coincidence, but by God. As a result, they produce a different kind of fear that results in reverence that causes us to run to God rather than run from God.

So right now, recall this part of your story. Do you remember the moment or moments you were frightened yet still stubborn?

PART TWO | A WARNED MAN

At last Daniel came in before me—he who was named Belteshazzar after the name of my god, and in whom is the spirit of the holy gods—and I told him the dream, saying, "O Belteshazzar, chief of the magicians, because I know that the spirit of the holy gods is in you and that no mystery is too difficult for you, tell me the visions of my dream that I saw and their interpretation. The visions of my head as I lay in bed were these: I saw, and behold, a tree in the midst of the earth, and its height was great. The tree grew and became strong, and its top reached to heaven, and it was visible to the end of the whole earth. Its leaves were beautiful and its fruit abundant, and in it was food for all. The beasts of the field found shade under it, and the birds of the heavens lived in its branches, and all flesh was fed from it. "I saw in the visions of my head as I lay in bed, and behold, a watcher, a holy one, came down from heaven. He proclaimed aloud and said thus: 'Chop down the tree and lop off its branches, strip off its leaves and scatter its fruit. Let the beasts flee from under it and the birds from its branches. But leave the stump of its roots in the earth, bound with a band of iron and bronze, amid the tender grass of the field. Let him be wet with the dew of heaven. Let his portion be with the beasts in the grass of the earth. Let his mind be changed from a man's, and let a beast's mind be given to him; and let seven periods of time pass over him. The sentence is by the decree of the watchers, the decision by the word of the holy ones, to the end that the living may know that the Most High rules the kingdom of men and gives it to whom he will and sets over it the lowliest of men." This dream I, King Nebuchadnezzar, saw. And you, O Belteshazzar, tell me the interpretation, because all the wise men of my kingdom are not able to make known to me the interpretation, but you are able, for the spirit of the holy gods is in you.

— DANIEL 4:8-18

Into this baffling moment walks Daniel, the man of God, because that's what God does: he sends men of God to frightened men.

Sometimes these men pay attention, and sometimes they don't. But in the end, they are warned. Even Nebuchadnezzar knows that something is different about Daniel, *"that the spirit of the holy gods is in him."* While Daniel is governed by Babylon, re-educated in Babylon, and renamed after a Babylonian god, he remains resolute. He is directed by the Spirit of God and remains unaffected by the spirit of the times so he can warn the world's most powerful man.

Daniel does what he is supposed to do again: he interprets another one of the king's dreams. The interpretation is obvious. Nebuchadnezzar has grown an incredible canopy of wealth and power. It's majestic, and it covers the earth. But God is going to come down and chop that canopy down. He is going to strip it bare. People under it are going to run. All that's going to be left is a majestic stump.

You know what this dream is. It's a nightmare. It's a nightmare for the man who has established his wealth and power with no thought of God. It's a nightmare for the man who has built a career, established a name, developed assets, and has given every day to thinking only of himself. Know this: Nebuchadnezzar has built more fame, splendor, success, and wealth than any man ever will. He had more wealth than Elon Musk, Jeff Bezos, Bill Gates, and Warren Buffett combined. He was a world emperor. There was no one like him. And guess what? God is warning him that he is going to show up with a giant chainsaw and cut him down like the sapling he is to him.

74

So right now, recall this part of your story. Do you remember the moment that God was warning you?

PART THREE | AN ARROGANT MAN

The tree you saw, which grew and became strong, so that its top reached to heaven, and it was visible to the end of the whole earth, whose leaves were beautiful and its fruit abundant, and in which was food for all, under which beasts of the field found shade, and in whose branches the birds of the heavens lived— it is you, O king, who have grown and become strong. Your greatness has grown and reaches to heaven, and your dominion to the ends of the earth. And because the king saw a watcher, a holy one, coming down from heaven and saying, 'Chop down the tree and destroy it, but leave the stump of its roots in the earth, bound with a band of iron and bronze, in the tender grass of the field, and let him be wet with the dew of heaven, and let his portion be with the beasts of the field, till seven periods of time pass over him,' this is the interpretation, O king: It is a decree of the Most High, which has come upon my lord the king, that you shall be driven from among men, and your dwelling shall be with the beasts of the field. You shall be made to eat grass like an ox, and you shall be wet with the dew of heaven, and seven periods of time shall pass over you, till you know that the Most High rules the kingdom of men and gives it to whom he will. And as it was commanded to leave the stump of the roots of the tree, your kingdom shall be confirmed for you from the time that you know

*that Heaven rules. Therefore, O king, let my counsel
be acceptable to you: break off your sins by practicing
righteousness, and your iniquities by showing mercy to
the oppressed, that there may perhaps be a lengthening
of your prosperity.*

— DANIEL 4:20-27

Daniel's interpretation is interesting because it's a prophecy, a historical event, and a parable of how most men live life. Here's the parable: we start by trying to do life our way. We are in the leader's seat. When we encounter that our way doesn't work or isn't going to work forever, we come to a moment of decision: either we're the leader of our life, or God is. There cannot be two leaders. Either he's the King of my life, or I am. He's the Lord of my life, or I am. He's the Savior of my life, or I am.

Then, right at the end, Daniel offers Nebuchadnezzar some free advice. It's wisdom he adds based on the interpretation. *Repent*. He essentially says:

"Man, brother, I have walked with you for about 30 years. And you have gained it all. The world is at your command. But you will die one day, because you are not a god. But you can know one. He is the one true God, the Highest God. He gave you this dream to warn you to stop sinning and start living righteously. So why not live this last part of your life even better than the first?"

The reason for the dream was not to entertain Nebuchadnezzar. The reason for the dream was not just to predict the future and have Daniel interpret. The reason God gave him the dream was to warn him that his arrogance had gone too far. The king did not heed the warning.

Listen to what happens just one year later.

> *At the end of twelve months he was walking on the roof of the royal palace of Babylon, and the king answered and said, "Is not this great Babylon, which I have built by my mighty power as a royal residence and for the glory of my majesty?"*
>
> **— DANIEL 4:28-30**

For 30 years, God had been warning Nebuchadnezzar! He gave him numerous warnings. We have read of at least three insistences in Daniel. The first warning came with a dream of his empire being destroyed. Then next, three men were saved by God from the fury of his rage and were unscathed by the fiery furnace. And last, God gives him a final warning through this dream here. Daniel even pleads with him. God warns and waits to see how he will respond. God gave him a lot of time. After the last warning, he gives him another whole year. But again, left to himself, we see his selfishness is too deep. From his own words we learn he is too intoxicated with his accomplishments, might, and majesty. His unrelenting arrogance is drunk on himself. He is resistant to God because in his mind, he has become a god.

God is always calling arrogant men to obedience. He gives them ample time to repent. More time than we would because he is far more patient than we are. But his warnings and patience do have an end. On the other side is destruction for even the greatest of men because no man is as mighty as God. What's about to happen to Nebuchadnezzar is a sobering reality for ungodly men.

So right now, recall this part of your personal story. Do you remember the arrogant man you were—or might still be?

PART FOUR | A DEAF MAN

While the words were still in the king's mouth, there fell a voice from heaven, "O King Nebuchadnezzar, to you it is spoken: The kingdom has departed from you, and you shall be driven from among men, and your dwelling shall be with the beasts of the field. And you shall be made to eat grass like an ox, and seven periods of time shall pass over you, until you know that the Most High rules the kingdom of men and gives it to whom he will." Immediately the word was fulfilled against Nebuchadnezzar.

— DANIEL 4:31-33

What we see here is one man who refused to listen to God's Word and was driven crazy as a result. So, just because a man doesn't have a Bible in his hand or a church in his area, he is not excused. God speaks to men in numerous ways. God can speak however he likes and in any way he likes. After all, he is God. In the case of Nebuchadnezzar, God is going to use dreams to pierce the walls of his impenetrable palace, into the reaches into his seemingly impenetrable heart. Therefore God is always speaking, calling, and reaching out to men. He calls to men through events, dreams, circumstances, and even his people. He presents everyone with warnings giving us numerous opportunities to believe, just like he did here. Nebuchadnezzar is given dreams, visions, explanations, miracles, and people (*note*: not a Bible or a church). Yet he rejects them all.

This is the case for all men. God is speaking and warning us all that he is God. He did it this way long before the Bible was ever printed on a press. He did it long before denominations ever existed. He gave all men opportunities to hear and believe even when they were surrounded by pagan ideas, pagan politics, and pagan gods. All men are without excuse.

The question is not, *"Is God speaking?"* The question is, *"Are you listening?"* Are you hearing God and heeding his voice? Because at some point, all men will meet with the terror of his mighty voice. And you want to make sure that it's not the first time you've heard it because, at that moment, it's too late.

So right now, recall this part of your story. When you were deaf to God, what event, dream, miracle, person opened your ears to hearing and heeding God?

PART FIVE | A SURRENDERED MAN

At the end of the days I, Nebuchadnezzar, lifted my eyes to heaven, and my reason returned to me, and I blessed the Most High, and praised and honored him who lives forever,

for his dominion is an everlasting dominion,
and his kingdom endures from generation to generation;
all the inhabitants of the earth are accounted as nothing,
and he does according to his will among the host of heaven
and among the inhabitants of the earth;
and none can stay his hand
or say to him, "What have you done?"

At the same time my reason returned to me, and for the glory of my kingdom, my majesty and splendor returned to me. My counselors and my lords sought me, and I was established in my kingdom, and still more greatness was added to me. Now I, Nebuchadnezzar, praise and extol and honor the King of heaven, for all his works are right and his ways are just; and those who walk in pride he is able to humble.

— DANIEL 4:34-37

This is an incredible moment. A lot of people will question how genuine this is because we have seen Nebuchadnezzar flip-flop many times before. The simple answer is that we don't know because this is the end of the narrative about him. It's all we have. I like to believe it is genuine. Otherwise, Daniel would not have completed his narrative about him this way.

What we know is that Nebuchadnezzar is portrayed as the greatest villain in the entire Bible. His wickedness is referenced in six different books of the Bible, and he is described as vehemently opposed to God every time. But here's the deal: saved or not, we don't need to worry about this. This unsettled issue of the past is not the most significant question.

The bigger question is this: Do you believe that God is God? Will you surrender to him and let him be King, Savior, and Lord of you? That's the only question that matters. It's the only one that needs to be answered.

So right now, recall this part of your story. When was that moment you surrendered to God? Recall it. Remember it. And share it.

If you have never done that, you can do that today. You can make that decision now and stop fighting with the God of all Gods. You can proclaim him King of Kings and Lord of Lords and let him lead your life today. You will have to surrender doing life your way and do it his way—forever. If you are ready to do that, you can make that decision right where you are today.

John 1:12 states:

> *"But to all who did receive him, who believed in his name, he gave the right to become children of God."*

There are probably a couple of outcomes. For some men, this might be the moment they surrender to God for the first time. For other men this might be a reminder to come back to God, who is always calling men. For still others this might be a reminder to you that God wants to use men like you to tell his story and how he has worked through you: a frightened, warned, arrogant, deaf, and surrendered man.

As we conclude this study I want you to know I have loved getting to know Daniel with you. If you ever want to reach out to me, you can always do so. And if you want to continue meeting daily, you can join me as we read through the Bible on the Men's Daily Devo.

And remember live all-in for him who lived all-in for you.

REFLECTION & DISCUSSION QUESTIONS

- Have you decided to surrender to God? When and where?
- Which of the five parts of Nebuchadnezzar's journey did you most connect with as relates to your own spiritual journey?
- How has this session helped you in knowing how to share your story?